Cheryl Cole

through my eyes

CORGI BOOKS

For me, looking at pictures is a bit like listening to music. It reminds you of what you were doing and how you were feeling at certain points in your life. I can look at photos and straight away they will bring back all kinds of memories.

When it came to choosing the pictures for this book, I went for a real mixture. Some are from big occasions in my career, like the Brits and the Cannes Film Festival, and some are my personal photos taken behind the scenes, of me preparing for things or of me just relaxing on a day off. All are times and places that I'd like to share with you.

Sometimes I look at pictures and can't believe it's me. I think we probably all have those moments when photos aren't anything like the way we see ourselves. I seem to change all the time. With photo shoots, so much depends on the lighting, makeup, hair, the photographer, whether it's in a studio or on location and what kind of mood you're in on that day. It all comes through in the pictures. I love the personal photos, the informal ones.

Putting this collection of pictures together was an opportunity to take another look at some of the amazing experiences I've had. Things sometimes happen in a bit of an adrenalin haze so it's nice to enjoy those moments again at my own pace. I wanted a book that was packed with memories. I hope you enjoy it.

Love,

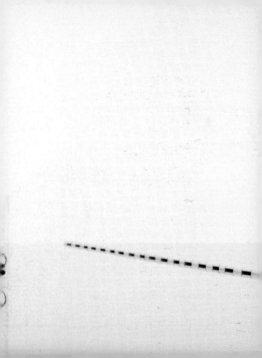

In 2009, we decided to take a break from Girls Aloud. During this time an opportunity came for me to make a solo album. Music and performing has always been my biggest passion, so this seemed like a natural step. I never plan where I want to be or what I want to be doing in the next five or ten years … I believe everything happens for a reason.

Even when I was a kid I somehow knew I was meant to be some kind of entertainer. I was always singing and dancing. It was all I was interested in, it was my dream. I never considered anything else.

Going solo after seven years with the girls was scary and exciting at the same time – but it definitely felt like the right thing to do. I was going back to the start and had to establish myself as a solo artist but I had the experience I'd gained from the girls to draw on.

I did a lot of the recording for my album *3 Words* in LA, as a lot of the producers I was working with are based out there. Will.i.am from the Black Eyed Peas was the executive producer on the album and was also a huge influence on me going solo. We first met in 2008 when I appeared in the video for his single 'Heartbreaker' and we got on straight away. I find him inspiring. He is a musical genius – everything you'd want from a producer and a person: creative, fascinating, intelligent, fun to be with. When I'm with him I feel like I'm learning constantly. He's a very special person, passionate to the core about what he does, and grateful for what he's achieved. I don't think he actually realizes how far he's come. He's very humble, and it was just easy writing and making music with him. Working with him is an absolute honour – I would work with him for the rest of my career if I could. I wrote four of the tracks on *3 Words* with him and for the others it was a case of listening to loads of stuff and picking what I liked.

I remember really clearly going into the studio for the first time to work on my solo material. I was with Will so it was all a bit nerve-racking. Actually, I was terrified. The track was 'Heaven', the first song I'd ever written with him, which was scary enough, then it was a case of learning how he works. I was so nervous. I remember thinking, Oh, God, I hope he likes what I've done and this turns out all right.

It was just a case of getting on with it: I wanted to do the album and I couldn't have had anyone better to work with so I had to overcome my fear. He knew exactly how I was feeling and was great with me.

I've spent a bit of time in LA over the past couple of years and I really like it. It's amazing what a difference it makes when there's a bit of sun and you're in a new environment. If I woke up in my bed at home and got up to go into the studio knowing I was coming back at the end of the day I'd feel completely different. It's strange, but being out of my comfort zone is definitely a good thing, and I love it that the sun shines all the time. Who wouldn't?!

Even though I like it there and enjoy experiencing new places, I'm a real home person, so when I'm away I miss loads of things – just my cups of tea, that kind of ordinary everyday stuff. I miss the dogs like crazy. I used to talk to them on the phone but I don't now because I've discovered they're not interested. They don't listen!

I'm a creature of habit and I like to know where I'm at, what's going on, so it was weird to be working with new people on my album and not have the girls around. With GA material we'd talk to each other and get enthusiastic about songs; there'd always be somebody buzzing about. I'd also worked with Brian Higgins, who produced all our albums for seven years, so that was a huge comfort zone to step out of – I had to get to know new producers. At the same time, it was all fresh and exciting and challenging. It was a buzz.

In the past I'd co-written Girls Aloud album and B-side tracks but it was totally different doing my own stuff. I'd say it's more the kind of music I would listen to at home. The lyrics tend to reflect what I'd say about subjects I feel strongly about, so generally it feels more personal. I love what we've done with Girls Aloud so far and the British pop sound we're known for. We had a very specific formula – quirky lyrics, songs that sometimes didn't have choruses – so what I'm doing now is different. My solo material's a little bit less pop and more urban-sounding.

The album was released in October 2009 and I couldn't believe that it went straight to number one, I was amazed. It still hasn't sunk in that it's gone triple platinum – I have the disc at home but it still doesn't seem real!

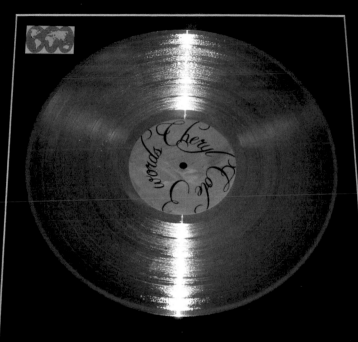

Presented to

CHERYL COLE

to recognise Worldwide sales of
over 1,000,000 copies of the

FASCINATION

album

'3 WORDS'

2009

The first single, 'Fight For This Love', was written for me by Steve Kipner, Wayne Wilkins and Andre Merritt. I recorded it with Wayne in his studio in Santa Monica. He's English but now lives out in America. It was a really good experience, we really hit it off. He's just brilliant, so easy to record with – not scary or intimidating at all. I worked with him on the second album too.

When I first heard 'Fight' I found it very empowering because the lyric is so strong. It's got that feisty thing going for it. It seemed to sum up the way life can feel like one big fight sometimes and you've got to push your way through.

At that stage I wasn't thinking of it as the first single. While I was recording the album, everything was new for me, and it was only when the whole thing was completed and I was getting reactions from other people that I knew it was the track I wanted to release first.

With every song I have a picture in my head of how I want to perform it. I wouldn't be drawn to a song or feel like I'd connected with it unless I had that vision. When you're in the studio recording it's not just about singing, you're actually performing and capturing the emotion of the song, and that's what comes across when people listen to it.

When it came to the 'Fight For This Love' video it felt really odd being on my own and not having the girls around for support. 'Exposed' would be the right word. I was very nervous but I had a really cool director, Ray Kay, who has done some unbelievable videos with people like Lady GaGa and Beyoncé. I thoroughly enjoyed working with him. He's got a lovely calm vibe and he let me be free and be myself.

The dance scene in the video was really important to me. I liked that sense of being in a pack, right in the middle of the dancers, not out in front on my own, and Beth (Honan), my choreographer, came up with a routine that was just right. It's one thing knowing what you want but you need a good team to put your thoughts into action.

By the time we did the dance scene I'd been on set for a while but the nerves hadn't quite gone. I was full of adrenalin, heart pounding, and I could feel my fingers trembling. Plus, I was really unfit because I'd been so busy and there'd been no time to work out.

I love the way the video turned out. It felt really strong, just like the song, and the styling worked well. I have a lot of input in terms of what I wear and I go through ideas with Victoria (Adcock), my stylist. She creates what we call mood boards with lots of different looks and, based on those, I decide what I like. The red jacket was my favourite look, and from then on the military theme stayed and ran through everything I did right up to the tour in 2010.

When 'Fight' was released it went to number one. I hadn't dared to think about it doing so well so it was a lot to take in. Maybe when I look back in another year's time it won't feel so unreal.

The second single, '3 Words', was the duet with Will. For a long time that was my favourite track on the album because it was fresh and I had really good memories of recording it. I was just proud of it. I've realized, though, that it's impossible to pick out just one track and say, 'That's the one I like best,' because the way I feel changes all the time.

The video felt very different from anything I'd done before – not the kind of pop performance I was used to, it was very quirky and cool.

In terms of styling I had four quite distinct looks. In one scene I wore a long Edwardian skirt with a little bra top. I had white hair and we'd had a crystal veil specially made. In another scene my hair was up, my face was covered with a sheer veil, and I had on a simple Grecian-style dress with a big statement necklace. We did a scene with my hair loose and a wind machine blowing and I'd had a dress made with lots of chiffon at the back that billowed out. I also wore green contact lenses, which I loved, although I think some people got a bit freaked out by them! In total contrast to the dresses there was a quite robotic-looking, futuristic catsuit.

The director, Saam Farahmand, had this idea of split screens with the action coming together and then moving apart, so a lot of that went in at the editing stage. The single went to number four.

The next track to be released, on 15 March 2010, was 'Parachute', written by Ingrid Michaelson and Marshall Altman. It went to number five. When I first heard the track it just seemed to lend itself to ballroom. Straight away I knew I wanted to do a kind of edgy *paso doble* and stamp my feet. When I was young I did ballroom dancing, went to classes until I was ten, and it's something I've always loved and admired. I thought it would be perfect to have that kind of energy and that it would bring something different visually.

We needed to find someone who could bring my vision to life in the best way possible. My manager Hillary Shaw is very good friends with Bruno Tonioli, who is a judge on both *Dancing With The Stars* and *Strictly Come Dancing*, and he said he had the perfect person. That was how I met Derek Hough. He is a world champion of Latin and ballroom – the best there is – and was my choreographer and partner for the video 'Parachute'. I love his work and what he came up with was exactly what I'd envisaged. He's a sweetheart, the kind of person who makes the day more enjoyable, and that's really important when you're on set doing a video for eighteen, nineteen hours – maybe longer.

The location for the shoot was Eltham Palace, a beautiful old building
in south-east London that was perfect in terms of creating the romantic
and slightly old-fashioned backdrop I was after to go with the song
and the lyrics.

We always put a lot of thought into styling and for 'Parachute' we ended
up with three distinct looks. Because of the ballroom feel I went for a
flamenco-style dress, not traditional but quite Gothic-looking, and a one-
legged catsuit and a blouse and skirt for the other looks. It's really exciting
to dress up and get a feeling for how the whole thing is going to come
together. I've come to the conclusion you can never rehearse enough –
I always wish I had more time. It's only on the day when you're in costume
and the kind of heels that look stunning but are quite hard to dance in that
you get to work out how it's going to be.

'Parachute' is one of my favourite videos. Basically, it's the story of a relationship with someone who's there no matter what. It's set in a dream world and it's about reflecting on another time – so it's part dreaming, part reality and part reflection. It's quite a slushy song but, like all the others on the album, I definitely relate to it.

Videos are not as glamorous as you might think. A lot of it is about creating an illusion. In 'Parachute' there's a scene where I'm on a bed and you're not quite sure if it's all a dream. To get the right effect the directors, Alex Large and Liane Sommers, wanted it lit from underneath so the surface had to be see-through. It was actually a solid plastic platform. We did those shots at the end of a very long day. I think I'd gone into Hair and Makeup at five thirty a.m. and by then it was about ten thirty p.m. and I could feel myself going numb. It got to nearly midnight, we were on the last shot of the day, almost done, and all I could think about was getting into my pyjamas and slippers. Then the fire alarm went off and we had to clear the building. I ended up in the car in my dressing-gown while the fire brigade checked the place before giving us the all-clear to go back in and finish off. It was one of those 'be careful what you wish for' moments – I did end up in my night things, but I still had to go back and do that last shot. Not what I'd had in mind at all!

Slowly but surely I'm finding my feet, getting more used to making videos on my own. Parts of the process are easier as a solo artist – hair and makeup don't take as long – but some elements are harder. I miss the girls terribly but I'm definitely having a great time.

It's been exciting going to other countries. It just felt like a natural progression. Mind you, it can be a bit strange doing interviews when everyone around you is speaking a different language and you've no idea what they're saying! I was absolutely buzzing when 'Fight For This Love' went top ten in eleven countries and was a number-one hit in Denmark, Norway and Hungary. I haven't really wrapped my head round that yet. I'm just having fun with the music.

My second album *Messy Little Raindrops* was released in November 2010. In terms of style, I think it moved on a little bit from the first one. Again, it's a mix of tracks I've written and ones that have come from other writers.

I snatch time here and there to write, or schedule a day off. I do so much travelling I've got into the habit of writing on the plane, especially if it's a long flight somewhere.

One of the songs, 'Cold Heart', has inspired me to think about learning to play the piano. When I first got the demo it was a simple three-chord piano track and I'd love it if I could play it. I'm not making any promises but I like the idea.

THE X FACTOR

'Hold My Hand'

When I started on *The X Factor*, I felt like it was the perfect show for me, although it was definitely strange, surreal almost, being a judge, after I'd gone through that whole audition process just a few years ago.

I know exactly what it's like walking into the room, legs like jelly, and having to sing. You can see from the look on people's faces how much it means. At times, It's unbelievably intense. There's no escaping the fact that a single audition, which is over in a few minutes, could be the start of a process that changes your life for ever.

When I was asked to be an *X Factor* judge in 2008 I knew straight away I wanted to do it and, timing-wise, it felt perfect. By then I'd been in the industry six years and learned a massive amount, sometimes the hard way, and I really liked the idea of working with people who were just starting out. It was never about judging people, just about being honest and making constructive comments. My first day took me right back to when I auditioned for *Popstars: The Rivals*.

I absolutely love being a mentor, seeing talented people grow in confidence as the weeks go by. I just want to make sure I do the best I can for them. When it comes to the live shows, it's tough for them performing and maybe getting harsh comments, so I want my acts to know there's somebody who's always on their side. I'm always honest, and I don't mind telling people if they haven't performed to the best of their ability, but at the same time I'm incredibly loyal. Hopefully, I can help when the stress kicks in and it all gets a bit much. It's a lot to deal with, and some of the contestants are very young, so no wonder emotions tend to be all over the place. At times, it can be hard to hold it together. I find it incredibly moving to see the acts I'm working with pull off amazing performances under extreme pressure.

It was an absolute pleasure to work with Alexandra Burke, who won in 2008, and Joe McElderry, who won in 2009. Musically, they couldn't be more different, but in terms of character and temperament they're very similar – two of the nicest, most hard-working people you're ever likely to come across in the music business. I find it hard to put into words how much it meant to go through the whole experience with them. The chance to work with the likes of Alex and Joe, to play a part in helping them make it, was really why I was so passionate about doing *The X Factor* in the first place.

I like to fight for the people I'm working with and I make sure the song choices are right, that the styling works for them, that kind of thing.

Auditions start in June and the momentum builds all the way through to December, so by the time you get to the final it's consumed more than half the year. They tend to be long days while we're doing the auditions – twelve hours, more sometimes – with lots of travelling, and it can be quite draining. When it comes to the studio shows you have to be there four days a week, and the rest of the time you tend to be on the phone, just making sure everything's going the way it should. Some weeks can be more demanding than others, if there's a problem with one of the songs or the styling's not right, etc.

One thing I love about *The X Factor* is that all the judges are really different. For a start, we don't have the same taste in music and there's quite a range of ages. Our backgrounds couldn't be more different either. Louis is from management, Dannii's from a dance music and TV world, I'm from pop, and Simon's from a record label. The mix just works. We've all got our own personalities, our own opinions, and that means we're not going to agree all the time. Even during the audition process I can absolutely love somebody and the other three will be totally on a different wavelength. I think that's always good. If we all felt the same it would be boring.

When I joined the show, I didn't know what to expect and had no idea how much it would affect me. When I watched Alex doing her sound check with Beyoncé for the final that first year I cried my eyes out. I was crying the whole day. I mean, it was Beyoncé. You couldn't get a bigger star and I love her work. I knew how much it meant for Alex to be on that stage with her. It was written all over her face that she was totally overwhelmed.

It was incredibly nerve-racking waiting with Alex to find out who the winner was. I really felt for her, and for JLS, who were in the same boat with their mentor, Louis. As soon as Dermot said Alex's name I just felt her go, drop to the floor, and I literally pulled her back up. We were both euphoric, but at the same time she was so shocked she couldn't stop sobbing and shaking. She could hardly speak.

In 2009 Joe was in the same position, up there with the other finalist, Olly Murs, and Simon. When you look at the pictures you can see Joe's got his head down and his face is drained of colour. He'd started out as one of 200,000 people who'd come and auditioned and there he was, right at the end of the process. It was a massive thing. I remember Dermot saying they'd had more than ten million votes, which was just phenomenal. I had hold of Joe's hand and it was wet. Then Dermot said, 'The winner of *The X Factor* 2009 is ...' and there was this long, long pause. It was unbearable. I was thinking, Enough! Just say it – speak! Those thirty seconds really do feel like about three hours. It's, like, 'Why don't you just tell us?'

I don't think Joe could really take it in when he heard his name. He looked shell-shocked. I couldn't have been happier for him. I'd loved him from his first audition and I was so proud to see him succeed. He's a lovely lad, like a little brother, and a fantastic ambassador for Newcastle, the part of the world we're both from, which made it even sweeter.

The X Factor was my first live performance of 'Fight' and the other act was … Whitney Houston. No pressure, then! It was completely mad on the day, a lot to take in, and I just kept thinking about how little time I had to dash from the judges' desk, get changed and be in position, all in the space of a four-minute commercial break. The timing had to be spot on and the slightest thing going wrong would have messed things up.

In the week leading up to the show I didn't have time to focus on what I was going to be doing, other than in the rehearsals, which I loved – seeing everything come together, choreography-wise and performance-wise, is always brilliant for me. I was much more focused on my acts and what they were doing. On the night, as soon as we were into the ad break that was it, I was off, and before I knew it I was up there. It hit me like a ton of bricks.

The whole experience was really terrifying, actually: I went from sitting with the judges to the stage and what felt like being judged by everybody else. It felt like everybody was anticipating the performance and how it was going to be and I was totally aware of that. I remember Simon winding me up, phoning the night before and saying something like, 'To be completely fair, Cheryl, you've done this to yourself. You've put yourself out there – it was your choice, your decision.' He was a bit sarcastic and said, 'Good luck with whatever happens,' just winding me up, really – although to be fair, ever since, he's always said he was really impressed.

When I think back those few minutes went by in a bit of a blur. It was quite crazy and emotional but I was glad to have a chance to thank everyone at *The X Factor* and the people who watch the show for making me feel so at home from day one.

I did a one-off special for ITV, *Cheryl Cole's Night In*, just before *The X Factor* final in December 2009. It was an amazing opportunity for me to bring together everybody I loved most in music at that point. Definitely one of the highlights: I got to perform '3 Words' with Will for the first time on TV. I think everybody knows how much I rate Will and that he's been a major influence on me, so to have him guest on my show was a real buzz.

I'm a massive fan of Rihanna, who's just such an original and edgy performer, so for her to come on and do 'Russian Roulette' was another very special moment. Snow Patrol, who I absolutely love, performed 'Run', and Will Young, who'd helped me during the Judges' Houses stage of *The X Factor* earlier in the year, sang 'Leave Right Now'. I felt incredibly proud watching Alexandra, who's grown so much as an artist since winning *The X Factor* in 2008, perform her number-one single, 'Bad Boys'. It was funny chatting with Alex to Holly Willoughby afterwards and thinking back to the year before.

I also got a chance to perform 'Parachute' with Derek Hough, who choreographed it. I loved the spectacle of that with the dancers and the whole Latin feel. I knew what I wanted to wear and I felt the flamenco-esque dress was perfect.

It was all really dramatic and made me feel like a proper ballroom dancer just for that one performance. It was the first time people had seen me like that and it was great to be able to do something so different.

Coco & Buster

I love spending time with my dogs, Buster and Coco. That's how I relax, just chilling out with them. They're Chihuahuas so they're only little, but they've got big personalities. I think Buster sees himself as lord of the manor and if I'm away and my mam takes him up to Newcastle it's like he's kingpin up there as well. Coco is nervous of other people so she follows me everywhere and looks to me for protection. She's my little baby.

The first year I did *The X Factor* I took Buster along quite a bit but he was so bad, weeing everywhere, even in the Green Room where everyone chills out. It was really embarrassing. Last year I took Coco with me and she definitely had better manners. In 2008 she had a puppy, Blue, and I wanted to keep him, but he was so naughty with the other dogs that in the end he went to Lily England, my PA, so I still get to see him. He's really good now, but whenever she brings him round to the house he turns into a little nightmare. He'll trot into the kitchen and wee to prove it's still a bit of his territory. I think that's definitely his way of winding up Buster. They don't actually fight but there's always a bit of a man-off when they get together!

'Crazy Butterflies'

In February 2010, just a few months into my solo career, I performed at the Brits. I'd been there in 2005 with Girls Aloud, when we were nominated in the Best Pop Act category, and again in 2008, when we were up for Best British Group. In 2009 it was a case of third time lucky when we won the Best British Single gong for 'The Promise'. We actually performed that night and, believe me, it was scary so I kind of knew what to expect when, a year later, I was back performing on my own.

The Brits are massive anyway, but 2010 was the thirtieth anniversary and it felt like it was even more of an event than usual at Earls Court. Literally the whole of the music industry was there. I felt privileged to be part of it, especially with 'Fight For This Love' nominated in the British Single category. That meant a lot. It really is amazing performing at the Brits. The weird thing is, you're aware of this huge event happening, all these artists coming and going, but at the same time when you're backstage getting ready you don't really see all that much.

During rehearsals I'd fallen over and hurt my knee. There was a bit in the routine where we all had to run up the stairs, and I'm not sure if somebody stood on the back of my coat or what, but the lights went off and I fell up about four stairs and banged it. I'd hurt the same one on tour so I was worried.

Before I went on I was in my dressing room and I could hear all the other acts performing. I just remember doing this countdown until it got to Jay-Z and Alicia Keys, and thinking: Right, I'm on next. I was waiting at the side of the stage as they were coming back down the stairs and it kind of brought home how big a deal it was. Jay-Z! I was feeling a mixture of emotions, excitement, and butterflies in my tummy too. In the back of my mind I knew millions of people would be watching, but I was trying not to think too much about that. Live TV is always terrifying, and there's nothing like the Brits to ramp up the nervous energy.

We'd made some changes to the routine for 'Fight For This Love' and put a remix, 'Show Me Love', in the middle, just to make it a little bit special for that one performance. It was all about strength. The production was risky in some respects, with forty dancers, stairs and a costume change halfway through. There was plenty of scope for things to go wrong, but you just have to go for it.

The opening was quite complicated as well. I came up from under the stage on something called a toaster, which actually pops up. I'd seen Michael Jackson do it in *This Is It* and it's quite a scary prop, but I remember being excited that I was going to get the opportunity to do the same move. I popped up really fast and did a jump, and had dancers coming up either side of me. In fact, they had more problems than I did because it was difficult to get the timing right for them to pop up together. I'd been worried about the knee I'd injured, that something would happen during the performance, but it was fine.

The costume was a custom-made trench coat, short at the front and long at the back, designed by my stylist Victoria Adcock and made by Stevie Stewart, and Ray-Ban Aviators. It's not as hard as you might think to dance in dark glasses, as long as the lights are really bright. The trench coat was a different take on the 'Fight' outfits, but keeping the military feel we'd gone with all along, which was what I wanted. Underneath, I had on a sparkly hooded body that had been specially made by Vicky Barkess, a designer who does fantastic dance stuff.

It really helped that I'd performed 'The Promise' at the Brits in 2009 with Girls Aloud. The five of us were so scared that night it was ridiculous. Again, it was a huge production number – more stairs, everyone worried about falling over in their high heels, and feeling the pressure of performing in front of all the bigwigs in the music industry. We'd done arena tours and played the 02, so it wasn't like we weren't used to complicated stage shows and big venues, but the Brits still had us quaking in our shoes. It was crazy but so exciting to win a Brit for Best British Single with 'The Promise' after seven years together. The fans voted for it, too, which meant a lot. That was a great night. A year on I could feel some of those nerves again and I definitely missed the other girls, although Kimberley and Nicola were in the audience.

It's a very different feeling going out there on your own. You definitely can't do it without some support, a kind of security blanket, and these days, that comes from my dancers. A few months back someone called them 'Cheryl's army' and it stuck. I always have Layla

on one side and Dominique on the other. I love them, and we've got that closeness so when we're on stage I can look at them and know exactly what they're thinking.

Performing at the Brits 2010 is something I'll never forget.

Around the time of the Brits I was starting to work on material for my second album, writing and recording, and a last-minute slot came up at the studio in LA. It meant flying out the day after the awards, first thing, so as soon as I came off stage I got changed, didn't make it to the record-company party at the Mandarin Oriental Hotel, just went straight home to pack. I was up most of the night and off to the airport early.

When I got to Heathrow there were one or two paparazzi and I was snapped on my way to Departures. I didn't think too much of it until I got to LAX. Lily was travelling with me and we picked up our luggage, then headed for the exit. Twelve hours on a plane, plus the time difference, means your body's a bit messed up and you're not exactly feeling a hundred per cent, so it didn't help to round a corner and come face to face with a wall of photographers. Before we even knew what was happening they'd rushed forward and surrounded us. There were probably fifty of them, some with video cameras, all pushing and yelling: '*Cheryl! Cheryl! What's happening?*' I'm five foot three, and not exactly a big build, so it was really intimidating. I actually got very scared. I hung on to Lily, and the two guys who were there to meet us somehow managed to force their way through, get hold of us and drag us through the crush to the car.

The paparazzi can be really scary. There's nothing you can do but put your head down and try to keep moving. You feel like you're being suffocated.

I managed to get into the car, but there were so many people around us that Lily was stuck and couldn't get in on her side. Some of the paparazzi had yanked open the other back door and were snapping away so she had to get in with me and, as you can see, the two of us ended up squashed into the same seat. As we drove away, I was shaking and could feel the adrenalin pumping. It was complete madness. I don't think you ever get used to it. It was only at the hotel, after we'd gone in the back way through the underground car park, and I finally got to my room and closed the door, that I started to feel calm again.

A week later, when I came back to London, it was even worse. I was inside the airport on the walkway and saw a TV crew and photographers. The police were there and I could feel myself beginning to panic because I knew straight away what I was about to walk into. Outside, there were masses of paparazzi and it was a crush just getting to the car. You can hardly see me in some of the pictures – just the top of the little brown trilby I had on.

I don't think people or even the paparazzi realize how scary it is to have all these big men pointing cameras, screaming in your face, screaming your name, screaming different things at you. If it wasn't for the guys who meet me and get me through in one piece I don't know what would happen. Even if they just stood back a bit, so I could get into my car safely and securely, it wouldn't be so bad – but they're in my face, in my car. I know they're just doing their job but I wish they'd respect my space. I should at least be allowed to breathe.

CHARI

'No Walk I
The Park

When I said I'd join the Comic Relief expedition to the summit of Mount Kilimanjaro in March 2009, I knew that getting to the top of Africa's highest mountain – 19,341 feet at its peak – would be a massive challenge. It was the hardest thing I've ever done in my life. I'd never been through anything that was so mentally and physically draining. I really have no idea how I kept going day after day.

Looking back, I don't think I appreciated just how taxing it would be. You can only prepare so much, and there's no way of knowing what a climb like that is going to do to you until you're actually out there and going through it. I felt like I was pretty fit anyway because I'd been busy with Girls Aloud. We'd been promoting the new album, *Out of Control*, and not long before I was due to go to Tanzania we performed at the Brits so I was in really good spirits. I definitely felt strong enough and fit enough for Kilimanjaro.

We'd been told it would take us nine days to reach the summit, walking ten, eleven hours a day, and I was fine with that. It wasn't actually the walking that was the tricky part – what knocks you for six is the freezing cold and the altitude. Even though you know the air is going to be thin and you've been told what it can do to you, it's impossible to imagine how it feels until you experience it. The sheer tiredness and lack of oxygen is just horrendous. I hadn't realized how cold it would be either.

For the first couple of days on the trek I felt okay, but then the altitude started to kick in. It made me nauseous and dizzy and my head was banging. You can see I'm crying tears of exhaustion in this photo. The whole thing was very emotional. Kimberley suffered as well. We were sharing a tent and trying to keep each other going. Every night it was a relief to climb into it, but I don't think any of us got any proper rest because the higher you go the worse you feel, and it's hard to breathe when you're lying down. I think most of us in the group battled different things at different times but we all wanted to keep going and get to the summit. The fact we were raising money to help prevent malaria, a disease that kills a child every thirty seconds in Africa, was a massive incentive.

I feel so lucky
that Kimberley
and I climbed
Kilimanjaro
together. I'd
never have
made it to the
top without her.

I was exhausted
when I finally finished
the Kilimanjaro expedition
but was so proud of what
all of us had achieved in
the long run.

When I got home there wasn't much time to rest and recover because there was a Girls Aloud tour coming up and we were about to go into rehearsals. I just took a couple of days to lie on the settee and eat whatever I wanted, and I seemed to be okay after that, except I had problems with the nail on one of my big toes. It fell off while we were doing the Out of Control tour when I was dancing in heels every night, which was really painful.

Almost a year after Kilimanjaro, in January 2010, there was another fundraising event, this time for the victims of the earthquake in Haiti. It was staggering to think that as many as 300,000 people had died and more than a million were left homeless by the disaster – heartbreaking to see the TV pictures showing the devastation. Simon Cowell decided to do a charity single, a cover of REM's 'Everybody Hurts', and got together lots of artists – from Mika to Take That and Rod Stewart – and less than two weeks after the quake struck, the record was being made. It was done in West London at Sarm Studios, which seemed the right place since that was where the

Band Aid single, 'Do They Know It's Christmas?', was recorded in 1984. They'd had everyone in Studio One at the same time, but for the Haiti single we all came in separately and I was one of the first.

It was a real privilege to be asked to take part. The response from the public was overwhelming and more than 450,000 copies were sold in the first week, sending it straight to number one. The proceeds went to the Disasters Emergency Committee and the *Sun*'s Helping Haiti campaign.

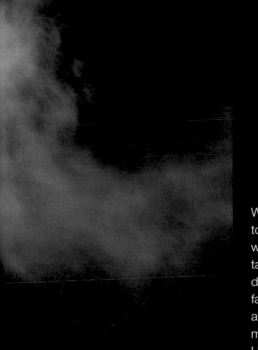

When we did the video shoot the idea was to create a kind of dust-storm effect so there were wind machines blowing a cloud of talcum powder. I had a few butterflies that day too, working with Joseph Kahn, a really famous director. He's collaborated with just about every big name you can think of in the music industry – 50 Cent, Black Eyed Peas, U2, Mariah Carey, Destiny's Child … The list just goes on. He had a really good vibe and the shoot was an absolute pleasure.

I did come away with a bit of an unusual souvenir, though – talc! I had a little black dress on that day and by the time we'd finished I was covered with it, head to foot, from the 'dust storm'. I had to do a quick change and get cleaned up because 'Fight For This Love' had been released in Europe and I was going straight to the airport for a flight to Vienna and a packed promo schedule when I arrived.

'Rain On Me'

Harper's

BAZAAR

June 2010 £3.99
www.harpersbazaar.co.uk

CHIC IN THE HEAT
5 WORK TO WEEKEND STYLE SECRETS

VENUS RISING
CHERYL COLE

MUST-BUY
THE NEW TRENCH DRESS

GET SEXY SUMMER LEGS

Fashion's EXOTIC
new mood

JE T'AIME
WHEN BIRKIN MET GAULTIER...

As well as my music and *The X Factor*, a huge part of what I do involves photo shoots.

It's a real honour to be offered covers of iconic magazines like *Vogue*, *Elle* and *Harper's Bazaar*. I'll be doing the shoot, wearing some amazing designer piece, and thinking, I can't actually believe it – especially not when I remember the kind of covers I was doing when I first started out with Girls Aloud. It just seems completely mad.

I've worked with some really famous photographers and directors, like Nick Knight, who did the album cover for *3 Words*, and Jake Nava, who shot one of the L'Oréal ads, and it's a privilege to work with people of that calibre.

I know it might sound strange but I'm not into photography – it's not something that excites me in the way music does – so I tend not to enjoy photo shoots. I'm not a model and that's probably why they don't fulfil me. I don't like staring at myself in static poses, but I have to do it and I've got better at it, I think. I'm learning all the time about how to make the process easier for myself, connecting with the camera, and making the pictures better so it doesn't look like I'm always smiling – which is the natural thing to do when a camera comes out. I don't want to look the same in every photo and I'm beginning to realize that you can end up looking totally different from one shoot to the next.

The way the pictures turn out comes down to lots of different elements. At the session I did for *Q* magazine, which was for these pictures in the rain, I had somebody doing my makeup who doesn't normally do it. The lighting also changes how you look. They are really grungy pictures, and I like the fact they are so different from any others I've done.

Every little thing contributes to the end result, and what's really odd is that how you *feel* on the day comes across in some pictures. What's going on inside gets captured.

I don't actually know what I look like any more – I see so many pictures of myself all the time. Sometimes I'll look at a picture and say, 'Is that actually me? Do I really look like that?' I rely heavily on the team around me, people I trust, to say if a picture looks good and why it works.

I take it as a real compliment to have nice things said about me, but I don't really get it when there's stuff in men's magazines about me. I'm not comfortable with the sex-symbol status. I have to see the funny side of being voted *FHM*'s Sexiest Woman in the World. I can't take it seriously. They obviously haven't seen me at home in my pyjamas, hair all over the place, and not a scrap of makeup on.

VOGUE

FEB
£3.80

Exclusive
**CHERYL
COLE**
The story
we all want
to know

**WORLD
WARDROBES**
Who's wearing
what where

David Bailey's
WOMEN
IN UNIFORM

**STYLE
AND
SENSUALITY**
How fashion is
rewriting the rules

Inside the life
and world of
**SAMANTHA
CAMERON**

FIRST LOOK
DESIGNERS' STAR PIECES FOR SPRING

When it comes to clothes, I haven't really got any favourite designers. If I'm doing a cover for a magazine like *Vogue*, the clothes tend to be really high-fashion pieces. I did a shoot for *Harper's Bazaar* in 2010, and some of the stuff was more like ornate art than fashion. There was an amazing mask covered in Swarovski crystals, which you can see here featured on the cover, and some stunning dresses that cost thousands. My favourite piece was a gorgeous little silver sequin jacket.

I'm not someone who loves shopping, mainly because I don't like the whole changing-room thing. For some reason the lighting's never all that flattering and it just makes you depressed, so I shop mostly online and try it all on in private at home.

This is one of my favourite
photo shoots. It was for
Glamour magazine.

In March 2010, we shot my 2011 calendar in LA. The pictures were going to be done in two very different locations – we had one day in the desert and another on the beach at Malibu. I think of California as a place where the sun always shines, so I never even wondered whether the weather might be an issue. I mean, it's LA, so it's guaranteed hot and sunny, right? Wrong! It was absolutely *freezing*. Every day in the week leading up to the shoot it was perfect: bright sunshine and boiling hot. The forecast for the days we had scheduled was rain and thunderstorms, so everyone was stressed and worried the whole thing would be a washout. We got lucky though and the rain held off and surprisingly the sun was shining. On the downside though, it was freezing and was blowing a gale – not what any of us had expected of LA in spring.

It looks really hot and sunny in this picture, but in reality I was freezing cold, even with hot air blasting through the heat funnel you can see here.

In the desert we were in an amazing place called the Easy Rest Motel.
It was built in 1990 on the outskirts of Lancaster as a set for a Dennis
Hopper film, *Eye of the Storm*. Apparently, when they finished shooting,
nobody wanted to tear the place down so it stayed, and it's been used
for quite a few other films, as well as photo shoots and music videos.

It was such a weird feeling to be in this battered old place in the middle of
nowhere. It had a real ghost-town feel about it with these spooky old motel
rooms and a diner called the Last Chance that looked like it had been
there about fifty years.

The photographers were Sandrine Dulermo and Michael Labica. I love their work and I always feel relaxed with them. They took the cover shot for this book! That day at the motel it was so cold they'd arranged for us to have heaters, but the ones we got made hardly any difference at all. We had someone standing just out of shot blasting heat from a huge funnel thing but you could hardly feel it.

The best thing was that I had one of those proper movie-star trailers to get ready in. I think it was used on the set of *King Kong* and it was just fantastic inside. At one end

there was a lounge and a kitchen, and at the other I had one of those makeup mirrors framed with lights, and rails for all the clothes. I absolutely loved it.

It was bitterly cold as well on the beach at Malibu, and the wind was blowing sand everywhere. As you can see here, I was completely covered with blankets from the waist down. The whole time we were working I could see the crew and my team in the background all wrapped up. Hillary even had her Uggs on! Later, they all said they felt like icicles but didn't dare complain as I was out there being blown about in all these tiny outfits.

For the last shot of the day I had to run into the sea. I was in high-waisted shorts, a little leather jacket, and some vintage cowboy boots. Even now, just thinking about it makes me shiver. I was frozen anyway, and the sea that day was like ice but I was actually giggling as we did the shot. It was one of those moments when if I hadn't laughed I'd have cried.

Looking back, I've got lots of happy memories of that shoot. It's strange because I hate the cold but I really enjoyed those two days. I'm much happier being outside in the fresh air than in a studio. You just feel a bit freer and you can enjoy it more. The pictures turned out really well. The colours and the amazing light mean it's worth braving the elements. I just need to remember to pack my Uggs next time …

Coconut is Sandrine and Michael's
dog. If I'm working with them in the
studio he's there, trotting in and out,
keeping an eye on what's going on.
It's always nice to have a dog around
the place.

ON TOUR

'Where I Belong'

Doing my first solo tour in 2010 was the best. I loved it. To be asked to support the Black Eyed Peas, pretty much *the* biggest band in the world right now, was the most incredible honour. I remember having a conversation with their manager and him saying, 'When you're the special guest on a tour, your role is to make the show the best it can be and to challenge the main act.' I thought, Okay, I'm up for a challenge. At the same time it was really daunting, knowing I had to go out there, prove myself and win over the audience, especially on the European dates when I wasn't sure how many people would know me.

I don't do anything in my life by halves so I didn't want to go out on stage with just a mike stand. We worked really hard to come up with something that was much more than a basic set. I knew the stage would be quite compact, that we couldn't go mad in terms of effects, and that I wouldn't be able to go off for costume changes, so it was a case of working within that. I did a thirty-minute set with three distinct parts to the show. They were Strength, Femininity and Independence, which represent my *3 Words*.

In terms of styling, I'd kept the military theme going since 'Fight' so I was looking for a way of carrying that through to the tour. I've always loved camouflage, that whole look.

I also went for the split trousers again, similar to what I'd worn to perform on *The X Factor*. They're so easy and comfortable to dance in. I love them and they've become a bit of a signature look for me. So, we went with camouflage for the opening section of the tour, Strength. This is a picture of me trying on my costume for the first time. I loved it and felt it was perfect to open the set.

For Femininity, I wore this one-shouldered dress, as I wanted something sheer and floaty. And for Independence, I had a studded white hooded dress and a pair of crystallized Ray-Bans. Actually, on the opening night I had a bit of a disaster with them …

This was me and my mam on the flight to Dublin for the opening night of the tour in May 2010. I was nervous but nothing ever bothers her. She's actually the most grounded person, like she's got a shield around her and things go straight over her head. I can be really hysterical and she's like, 'Calm down, what's wrong with you?' She's absolutely brilliant if I'm feeling the pressure, which I definitely was before that first night.

I could feel the buzz in the venue when we did the sound check in the afternoon. That's when it all starts coming together and you've got everyone busy getting the place ready. That first night I had the craziest butterflies ever. I got lots of good luck presents throughout the day, including a gift from Hillary – a dressing-gown with 'Cheryl On Tour' on the back – and flowers from the Peas. That made me a little bit nervous as I didn't really know all of them at that point, just Will. I was in my dressing room, thinking, God, they're really here, they're in this building, and I'm *really* on tour. I was excited as well: I wanted to get out there and do it because I'd been rehearsing for so long.

There were 14,000 people in the arena and I could feel my heart pounding, adrenalin racing through my body – just every emotion you can imagine. I put on my headphones and listened to some music, just got into a bit of a performing zone, and that helped. My dressing room is my little space where I can have a bit of quiet time and relax. On the road, I always have a kettle with me so I can make some tea and I light a couple of scented candles to make the place feel more homely, but that's about it. I don't have the room painted or anything!

Before I went on I got together with the band and the dancers. I have this little ritual now where we go into a huddle backstage and they do this 'Cheryl's Army' chant that gets us all pumped up.

It was definitely a good feeling to get that first show under my belt. It pretty much went without a hitch until we got to the Independence section and I put on the crystallized Ray-Bans for 'Rain On Me'. It was the first time I'd worn them under the proper stage lights and they completely steamed up. I couldn't see a thing! I did the last two songs just peaking out of the underneath and the sides of the lenses!

A bit later, back in my dressing room, there was a knock on the door and all four of the Black Eyed Peas had come to say congratulations and that they were pleased I was touring with them. They were actually on their way to the stage when they popped in so I was really blown away. I couldn't have had a better experience than being around them. They're just the

loveliest people you could ever wish to meet. I got flowers from them in my
dressing room every night. I think because they've been there, supporting
different acts, they know what it's like and they just went out of their way
to be friendly and make me feel welcome.

We did two nights in Dublin, then it was on to the 02 Arena in London.
There's something about the 02 that makes it special. Every artist who
plays it says the same. The nerves were definitely there that night but I was
excited. It meant a lot to me to perform at such an iconic venue on my first
solo tour.

On the second night at the 02, Will came on for '3 Words'. I had absolutely
no idea he was going to pop up like that. It was a complete surprise. He'd
said he wanted to do it but I'd said he was crazy because it would spoil the

anticipation of him coming on later with the Peas. All those people in the venue were there to see them, and the build-up is part of the fun. He said he loved the track and wanted to support me, but I was like, 'Don't come on – let the audience wait and get their surprise.' He wouldn't listen and the next thing I knew there he was. I think it must have been written all over my face how pleased I was. It felt amazing, because even though I've been in the studio with him for hours, written songs and made videos, it's another thing to perform together. From then on some nights he'd come on and some nights he wouldn't. The band was primed just in case and so were the dancers because they had to be in a different place if he appeared, but it was always unpredictable. We just had to be alert and I genuinely never knew what to expect.

The Black Eyed Peas have been a big inspiration to me musically so getting to know them has been amazing. They're all such good people. It was a great vibe, just so much positive energy. Fergie's lovely – you've got to feel for her, being with the three boys all the time! I'd sometimes watch the Peas' show and think, I've just been on that stage performing. Then I'd be struggling to work out how I'd gone from singing their songs at home in my bedroom to supporting them on a European tour. Just bizarre.

I had a day off in Milan before we went to Berlin and I went for a stroll, did some sightseeing, and nobody recognized me. It was one of those rare days when you're totally anonymous. I was with Lily, Lisa Laudat, who does my hair and makeup, and Richard Jones, my tour manager. We found a lovely restaurant, and it was such a nice day that we sat outside. Will came, and we had a long, lazy lunch that probably lasted about three hours. We wandered round a bit more and found a traditional Italian ice-cream parlour – one of those places with every flavour you can think of.

I had four massive scoops and in the heat it was melting and running down my arm. It was a great day.

I wasn't really sure whether the European fans would know me but in some of the venues the reception was overwhelming. When I stepped on to

the stage in Paris it was one of those magic moments when I could feel the electricity in the place. The energy was fantastic and the audience was chanting my name, which was unbelievable. I can remember thinking, This is what I live for.

One of the best things about touring is that every venue I go to I get to meet the fans and talk to them, and they're just really cool people. It's quite overwhelming for me sometimes, because I can get caught up with what I'm doing and not think about how a track might inspire someone else. Then I meet them and they've got a story about how my album's helped them when they were maybe going through a hard time, and I find it really touching. To be honest, that's what inspires me. I totally get it because I feel the same when I listen to the music I love, so hearing their stories is a fantastic reminder of why I wanted to do this in the first place.

The tour was a big eye-opener for me in a lot of ways: with the girls, I was at the level where we were the main act, all the bells and whistles, the flying through the air, having a B stage, everybody there to see us. We'd done all that – and then I was back to being a support act, going to countries where people had never heard of me, the audience looking at me, like, who *is* this girl?

On tour with Girls Aloud it was quite chaotic before a show, with the five of us spraying perfume and clouds of hairspray everywhere. On my own I learned to prepare in a different way by putting on my headphones and zoning out. The whole experience was a steep learning curve, and I wanted to do everything the best I possibly could. It was great to be able to tour, just me as a solo artist, in new countries – very exciting.

I really didn't want it to end – and when it did, I had the tour blues big-time. You always feel like that, but this tour seemed really short and I wasn't ready to stop. I was just starting. After a few weeks of being on stage I was finally comfortable with the whole set: I knew when the audience was going to react, I was in the zone, and then … it all stopped, just as I was getting on a roll.

This was taken at the Dolder Grand Hotel in Zürich on the tour. It's just the most incredible place. The views are stunning and the design is really cutting edge, even though the building has a very traditional feel from the outside. There are gadgets for adjusting the lights and opening the curtains, and they've got things like televisions in the mirrors – very James Bond.

I performed at a digital
conference in Munich, Germany,
in January 2010, and Will couldn't
be there so I had a hologram
instead! It was strange because
it actually looked quite real ...

'Slide On My
Louboutins'

When I was asked to be the new face of L'Oréal in 2009 it was the biggest compliment ever. I've always used their products anyway, but never in a million years did I dream that one day I'd represent the brand. To begin with, the whole idea threw me. It just felt crazy.

When I did the first TV advert I was conscious of
all these bigwigs watching and waiting for this
one iconic line – 'Because you're worth it' – to be
delivered. It was a weird moment but I got a real
buzz from it. It's incredibly exciting to be a L'Oréal
girl, and one of the huge perks of the job is that
they send you all the new products! I feel thoroughly
spoiled. I've even got my own limited-edition design
hairspray, which I still can't believe!

When it comes to beauty tips, we're all individuals and everyone's skin is different, but I'd just say keep it simple and always wash your face and moisturize before you go to bed: your skin rejuvenates while you sleep. Don't ever go to bed with your makeup on because that's how you get spots. I've been using L'Oréal cleanser for years and I know it works well for my skin. Find out what suits you, maybe have a couple of products you like, then chop and change between them so your skin doesn't get used to the same things all the time.

I'm not into spa treatments or facials or anything like that. I'm just not into pampering at all. I don't find it pleasurable or fun or relaxing. I get irritated really quickly so after half an hour or so I'm thinking, I could be off doing this, that or the other.

I don't have a specific fitness routine but I'm always on my feet, always on the go. I've got a very active lifestyle and I enjoy working out, dancing, all of that. I don't like going to the gym and running on a treadmill, though. It's just not me.

My style has changed over the years and I tend to be a lot more dressy than I used to be. If I wear my scruffs that's how I feel – scruffy – so they're for sitting round the house when I want to be in something that makes me feel cosy. Your clothes reflect how you feel so I probably wouldn't wear casual things to a business meeting.

Basically, I just like clothes that make me feel nice. As I said earlier, it's not like I have my top five designers or anything. Where the dresses or shoes are from, or how I mix and match things, doesn't matter to me as long as I feel good.

When it comes to big occasions I find it quite easy to decide on a dress. I think you always know when you put something on and it works. Sometimes I can feel stressed if there are five or six dresses to choose from and I don't like any of them or none of them work. There might be a dress that looks great on a model in a picture: I'll put it on and it won't work because I'm short.

I don't have a wardrobe full of amazing dresses I've only worn once. A designer lends me a dress and it goes back afterwards. I couldn't spend an extraordinary amount of money on something I'm only going to wear once. Even if I treat myself and buy an expensive pair of shoes, there's no way I'd wear them just once. You might get people in the media going, 'Ooh, she's worn those shoes again,' but I'm really not bothered. I'm sure they've got things they wear more than once.

People read far too much into clothes and what they're supposed to mean. I'm not one of those people who wear a slogan T-shirt because they're trying to send out a message to the world. I just wear what I like – and I think that's the best thing anyone can do: learn what's you, find clothes you feel good in, and just go for it.

I can't allow myself to be affected by everyone else's opinion. They're entitled to think what they want and they might not like what I wear – but as long as I do, that's okay. As long as I feel good on the night I really don't care if some magazine wants to put a tick or a cross next to my outfit. It's just another person's opinion and that's fine but I wouldn't let it influence how I dress. Absolutely not.

'Every Day And
Every Night'

One of the things I love about my life is there's always so much going on. Sometimes it can get a bit crazy, like in May 2010 when for a few days the diary was even more packed than usual. I seemed to be on and off planes all the time, rushing from one place to the next.

I was about halfway through the tour with the Black Eyed Peas when I went to the Cannes Film Festival to do a gig. It was a really special time for me, and being there with all the buzz of the festival was just unbelievable. I'd read about Cannes when I was a kid and it conjured up Hollywood and all the glitz and glam of the movies. The day I was there it was beautiful and sunny. Everybody was a bit more relaxed and there was a nice atmosphere.

I had a business lunch with Hillary and Fawaz Gruosi, who owns the jewellery firm De Grisogono. They host one of the two main parties of the festival and I was doing the gig for them. We ate on the terrace of the Hôtel Eden Roc, a lovely spot with views out to sea.

This is me pointing at the beautiful view – I didn't realize the paparazzi were out on boats taking pictures from the sea!

From lunch I went to do the sound check. The way the stage was set up, the sea was to the side and in front of us, and as we were rehearsing the sun was starting to go down. It was breathtaking to go from playing arenas to that kind of setting. I remember thinking it was a really special moment.

After the sound check I got ready for a photo shoot with Italian *Vanity Fair* in the gardens of the hotel. There wasn't much time to have my makeup done and get my hair put up – less than an hour – and it was a bit of a scramble. I wore this gorgeous Cavalli dress.

Once we'd done the photos it was time for the red carpet – more pictures and interviews, mainly with European press. When I think back, that day was jam-packed, but I like being busy, and as long as I'm involved with what I'm doing I don't really notice if the schedule's crazy.

The gig was fantastic. I did the full set I'd been doing on tour and just had fun with it. It was an interesting audience as well. I remember seeing Lionel Richie at one point! When I came off I got changed and joined the party. Will was the DJ and he was fantastic. He's a music maker so it's second nature to him. I was up all night, which really isn't like me, but when you're caught up in the atmosphere and the music's great, it's four in the morning before you know where you are.

I had an early start the next day, considering I'd not had much sleep.
We had to leave to get to Nice for a flight to Belgium and the next date on
the tour. We actually flew by private jet because that was the only way we
could get to Antwerp in time.

I was really lucky to go back to Cannes the following week with L'Oréal for a film première. I squeezed that trip in between a gig at the Bercy Arena in Paris and the Radio 1 Big Weekend in Bangor, Wales. The première was what I'd call a *real* red carpet event, very grand. I had another fantastic dress to wear, the white Versace you see here, and even the paparazzi were in suits. I absolutely love these next two pictures where you can see all the fuss going on. It does feel intimidating to be in the middle of all that. You've got the paparazzi screaming, telling you to turn this way and that, and I just stand there thinking, What on earth am I doing here? How did I ever get here?

The funny thing about the première was that the film I was there to see wasn't to my taste at all. I'm not very good with violence – I can't even watch boxing on TV – and it was *really* violent. I was with Hillary and Lily, and the three of us literally had our hands over our eyes. I did think about getting up and sneaking off, but the actors were sitting right behind us, so we stayed and watched the whole thing. By the time the credits rolled it wasn't just the blood and gore on the screen that had me wincing – by then my shoes were absolutely killing me too!

From Cannes it was off to Radio 1's Big Weekend in north Wales. We got stuck in bad traffic on the way but in the end we made it with time to spare so it was fine. It was one of the hottest days of the year and the atmosphere was brilliant, everyone singing along. I'd been touring in Europe beforehand, so to get to Bangor and have thousands of people chanting my name was really special. I knew I was home. It was a fantastic gig. At one point I saw Prince William standing at the side of the stage behind the sound desk with Kate Middleton. It was the surrealest thing.

I have had the craziest past couple of years ever – probably some of
the best times of my life! Who knows what's in store for me in the future …
I can only hope for more of the same.

I want to thank you all for reading the book and I hope
you have enjoyed this journey with me.

Till the next time …

Big kisses and best wishes!

Love from me

ACKNOWLEDGEMENTS

Firstly I'd like to thank the most important people in all of this, you are the reason I decided to do this book – my fans. You are the reason I'm here and I thank you for sticking with us and supporting me through all the years... Maria Malone and Lily, thank you for helping me write this and thanks to Sarah Emsley and Pat Lomax for making this all possible! Michael and Sandrine, I love your work and love working with you – you're two of the few people who truly capture how I feel and look. And lastly, Hillary and Jodie – thank you for pulling this all together.